Citing Your References

(3rd Edition)

Thi

h.

A Guide for Authors of Journal Articles and Students Writing Theses or Dissertations

by
David P Bosworth
A.Dip.Ed., M.A., Ph.D

This handbook describes a frequently used, standardised method of referencing cited articles when writing for academic, professional or interfaculty journals. It is also a system for students preparing term papers, dissertations and theses.

It is an overall checklist for a wide variety of publications. The system, allows easy addition to an existing bibliography.

Always check details

1

Preface to the Third Edition

The first edition of this handbook appeared in 1992; the result of years of editing, writing (and supervising the writing of) academic articles, essays, dissertations, theses, ... All of which involve the use of other peoples' work. The need (academically, ethically and in order to remain legal) to cite these works was only, it seemed, vaguely understood. The ways in which citations were (still are) made vary enormously. Here is a style that is easy to use, consistent throughout the work and (bowing to the legitimate complaints of librarians) makes it easy to find the original.

Since the original publication there have been additions to the ways in which we search for references. People have told me they need information on, particularly, the use of CD–ROM and the Internet so there are suggestions on their use and how they can be 'written up' in a coherent fashion.

My thanks, once again, to all those who helped make this handbook so useful it keeps selling out! Specifically students who made suggestions to help them in their writing; Marian Armstrong of the Learning Resources Development Group (LRDG) who read and commented, in her usual meticulous way, on the original drafts and to Pat Williamson who provided useful comments on contemporary requirements.

As always, when writing something like this, material gets incorporated which, when first heard, made little or no impact. Over time this information gets incorporated into a way of working and now appears here. To all those unmentioned helpers, my thanks.

None of these helpers can be blamed for any shortcomings. In this edition I have made some 'cosmetic' changes and tightened up on the presentation but decided that it would serve no useful purpose to update the books I have used as examples (the technique is the same, whether the publication you're citing was published in 1904 or 2004).

David Bosworth Gilwern 2004

Contents

Must I have a Bibliography?

YES! Unless, of course, you have done the virtually impossible of not referring to, or quoting from, someone else's work. Books and articles are the raw material from which your work will originate.

All SOURCES you use should be acknowledged.

Not to acknowledge your references could be an infringement of copyright; it certainly admits to a lack of scholastic integrity.

Plagiarism is both illegal and intellectually dishonest. Altering a word here and there doesn't excuse you!

You can overcome the problem quite easily.

Whenever you DO use someone else's material in any way acknowledge it. A common method in use (and my favourite because it is so easy) is the AUTHOUR/DATE (sometimes called the HARVARD) METHOD.

It has the advantages of being
- easy to use however long the work
- in everyday use by *most* academic journals and universities, worldwide.

It also allows additions to your listing of your references (at the end of the work) as you go along. Putting the list in alphabetical order is very easy with most wordprocesors.

Should it be called
References or Bibliography?

A matter of semantics, really; and it may well depend on who the writing is intended for. Where you do have a choice consider the Shorter Oxford Dictionary's (1985) definition:
   "Bibliography: Systematic description of books, their authorship, printing, publication, editions, etc. (A book containing such details.) The literature of a subject."

Yours is, at best, a limited bibliography. But, given the Shorter Oxford's definitions of **References,** your listing might be better described as:
   "(4)…direction of attention to something… (5) A direction to a, passage etc where certain information may be found. (6) The act of referring a person to information or an explanation " (page 1276)

You are going to be listing references so that others can consult them

so it would seem sensible to list them in a bibliography.

ISSN and ISBN

Electronic information storage means that books and journals are frequently referred to by a number that can be read via its bar code. Using these numbers in bibliographies makes the main aim of a bibliography—others being able to find your references—easy. Booksellers can quickly locate (and order) a book if you know its code. You may not be specifically asked to include them in your bibliography but it makes sense to do so.

ISSN is the International Standard Serial Number and you'll find one on the front cover of most academic journals (which librarians call 'serials').

ISBN is the International Standard Book Number and, where there are hardback and paperback versions you'll find the book will have two ISBNs—one for each. (Also, a new edition will have a different ISBN from the original version.) ISBNs appear, with all the other bibliographic data, on the title sheet of the book.

It's a good idea to make a note on your record card of all the data on the title sheet of the book/journal as soon as you take it down from the shelves.

Your Bibliography will list
all books, articles (possibly conversations) that have been used or helped your writing in any way and will be in alphabetic order of author's surname (or of the first named author).

The sections of this book explain how it's done in different situations.

Keeping Records

Right from the start you'll do well to bear in mind that you're going to prepare a *Bibliography* listing your *References*.

Keep a file card (manually or on your computer) for each item you even look at.

Fill in information as you read then, if you do use a quote or reference from it, the data will be to hand.

Record Card Details

At the top of the card—the first thing you do—note the reference details as they will appear in the bibliography—copied from the book/journal or off-print.

Include page numbers of journal Items and for all quotations.

Add your notes in your usual way.

So, your card will have this information:

Authors(s) Date of publication Edition (or reprint) Title (book or article and Journal) Publisher Place of Publication
Journal Volume and Number and pages for the article listed
the ISSN or ISBN

Your notes in your usual style, (including page numbers for any direct quotations you copy out)

Make a card for *everything* you look at, even glance at—you never know If you will want to use the Information and it's always the one you didn't note down that's really important when it comes to the final write up.

Standard Layout for a Reference

There is a standard form that can act as a guide for setting out your bibliography. It's simplest for a book (not in a series) written by one person. The set up is:

> Surname comma Forename or initial(s) full stop bracket date Close bracket *title* in italic stop place of publication colon publisher Stop ISBN colon the international standard book number

For example, you mention a book in your essay (or thesis, or dissertation) so you'll need to add it to your references as shown in the box below:

Surname is sometimes upper case (capitals) but most publishers prefer the look of 'mixed' upper and lower.

Italic is shown by single underline on a typewriter

> Bosworth, Tony. (1993) *Motoring Tips: Money-saving advice for buying and running a car.* London: Piatkus ISBN: 0 85112 637

It's normal for second and subsequent lines to be indented

Use of upper and lower case copied exactly as on the book

Variations are dealt with under the different headings in this booklet.

> All the information you need for the listing will be on the title sheet of the book/journal—check it; record it as you read

Book Author

In the text you only put the author's name and the date of the publication. So, you might write:

"One of the most prolific writers about open and flexible learning, Lewis (1984) describes how the methods of tutoring...."

In the bibliography you will have to fill in the details. This particular reference, therefore, will be:

Note the punctuation.

> Lewis, Roger. (1984) *How to Tutor and Support Learners.* London: Council for Educational Technology (GET). ISBN: 0 86184125 5

Remember: it's normal practice to indent second and subsequent lines of citings.

Later, you write

"We want to make sure what we are doing in the classroom is successful. The many ways of ensuring the outcomes of teaching through open learning are developed Lewis (1985), who says.........."

This is the same Lewis who will be referenced, this time:

> Lewis, Roger. (1985) *How to Develop and Manage an Open–learning Scheme.* London: Council for Educational Technology (CET). ISBN: 0 86184 148 4

In the Bibliography these two references will be in chronological order of publication:

> Lewis, Roger. (1984) *How to Tutor and Support Learners.* London: Council for Educational Technology (CET). ISBN: 0 86184 125 5
>
> Lewis, Roger. (1985) *How to Develop and Manage an Open-learning Scheme.* London: Council for Educational Technology (CET). ISBN: 0 86184 148 4

Where someone publishes two, or more, pieces in a year we have to add (a), (b) and so on to the date — 1991(a), l99l(b), for example. This is most likely to happen with Journal articles — more details on pages 0 and 00.

Article Author

You will almost certainly use Journals to get a lot of your information—they are an up-to-date source, and ejournals on the Internet can give the very latest information.

If you write:
"In his review of educational technology Bosworth (1990) tries to show how today's multimedia has a lot in common with earlier individualised learning."

The Bibliography you will have to show:

> Bosworth, David. (1990) Stand up the Real Educational Technology: a personal review. *Learning Resources Journal.* Volume 6 number 2. June. Pages 43–47. ISSN: 0268 2l25

The page numbers of an article must be given

It's the Journal Title that's in italic(underlined)

Problems: *Volume* and *issue* number; there are lots of preferences so check carefully with whoever you're writing for. It can be:
Volume 7 Number 6
Vol 7 No 6
7.6
7 (6)   (or combinations with italic and bold text)!
Titles of journals often have agreed abbreviations.
You'll have to check with whomever you're writing for.

It's quite likely that you will come to see a particular writer as your main 'support'. You will want to quote from, and refer to many writings of this academic's. You do exactly the same as you do for any books—an example is on the next page.

Meanwhile …

> ### A Semantic Interlude
>
> Periodicals arrive periodically (and are also called serials since they form a series of periodicals). Academic periodicals (serials) are referred to as Journals. Magazine is a name given to other (generally considered less important) periodicals. Your references might come from any of these—think of them all as Journals.

Same Author—Several Articles

Listing a number of articles by the same author is simply a matter of adding a letter to the date when you mention it in your writing.

As well as writing *the article listed on the previous page (*Stand up the Real Educational Technology: a personal review for the *Learning Resources Journal),* I also wrote something later in 1990. If someone decides to mention both there could be a problem; since it is still referenced as (1990) there's a possible confusion so it is necessary to add (a) and (b) to the date. The first will be (1990a); the second (1990b) both in the text and the bibliography.

So, add (a) to the reference in the comment on the previous page:
"In his review ... ... Bosworth (1990a) ..."

then, when you mention him later in your article, you will have to write "According to Bosworth (1990b) Lord Asa Briggs defined Open Learning...." for the second one.

The full bibliography will look like this:

> Bosworth, David P. (1990a) Stand up the Real Educational Technology: a personal review. *Learning Resources Journal.* Volume 6 Number 2. June. Pages 43-47. ISSN: 0268–2125
>
> Bosworth, David P. (1990b). Open learning—Moving into the Mainstream. *Open Learning Systems (OLS) News.* Number 33. September. Page 11. ISSN 0269–9729

You could leave out 'number': just put 33

Another way is to put the name only once

> Bosworth, David P. (1990a) Stand up the Real Educational Technology: a personal review. *Learning Resources Journal.* Volume 6 Number 2. June. Pages 43-47. ISSN: 0268–2125
>
> ————————— (1990b). Open learning—Moving into the Mainstream. *Open Learning Systems (OLS) News.* Number 33. September. Page 11. ISSN 0269–9729

Neater, but it does require more setting up.

Quotations

There are often times when you'll want to use someone else's actual words. To do so without acknowledging the original is the worst form of intellectual plagiarism. Do it properly. You might write:

... Goodyear (1995) tells us "...so few people have enough direct experience of using telematics networks for professional...." (Page 45). I'm more of the Opinion ... *Note: the page on which the quotation appears in the original is given at the end, outside the quotation marks.*

The bibliography entry is exactly the same as any other reference where you're citing a Journal:

Goodyear, Peter. (1995) Situation Action and Distributed Knowledge. *Innovations in Education and Training International.* Page 45. London: Kogan Page. ISSN: 1355–8005

If you don't mention the author in the introduction to the quotation this has to be included with the page number at the end. In which case our example will become:

'I agree ... "...so few people have enough direct experience of using telematics networks for professional... ." (Goodyear, 1995, Page 45)'

Leaving out the bracket around the date makes this a bit tidier!

As a general rule quotations should not be long.

Many publications indent 'longer' quotations and make sure the page reference is at the end of the line, like this one:

Language can facilitate or hinder learning; Bentley (1994) says

"When we want to make sure that we say what we mean we need to work to a simple formula. First we need to think what we want others to hear. Then we have to think of the best, simplest, words to use to say it. Then we have to think of how we want to say it, and all of this we have to do before we speak." (page 57)

The listing for this in the bibliography has to be:

Bentley, Trevor. (1994) *Facilitation: Providing Opportunities for Learning.* The McGraw-Hill Training Series (Series Editor Roger Bennett). London: McGraw-Hill. ISBN: 0 07 707684 2

I have included the series editor; not essential but it could be useful to your reader

JOINT AUTHORS

When two or more get together to write a book or article we have to show
- that it was written by them all
- how your reader can get hold of a copy.

Computer databases need a 'key word' to find a reference. It is easiest to use the name of the first named author (called the senior author) as your 'search word'.

The book written by Terry Evans and Daryl Nation, for example, will be on the database under the senior author's name so the required form for the text for some people could say something like "I have been looking at the conclusions drawn by Evans (1989) and Nation when they say....."

My preference (since this looks as if there is another publication by Nation) would be to write:
"I have been looking at the conclusions drawn by Evans (1989) and his co–author when they say......"

There are, then two acceptable ways to list this in the bibliography. Writing in the traditional way, the reference would read

> Evans, Terry, and Nation, Daryl. (eds.) (1989) *Critical Reflections on Distance Education.* (Deakin Studies in Education Series). Lewes: Falmer Press. ISBN: 1 85000 463 3

Bringing the whole thing up–to–date and with computer–based searches in mind the first named author will be given pride of listing; your list will now read:

> Evans, Terry, (ed.) (1989) and Nation, Daryl. *Critical Reflections on Distance Education.* (Deakin Studies in Education Series). Lewes: Falmer Press. ISBN: 1 85000 463 3

Find out what the people for whom you're writing, prefer.

Had Evans and Nation written for a journal the reference would be just the same using the conventions for journals:

> Evans, Terry. (1989) and Nation, Daryl. Critical Reflections on Distance Education. *Journal of Educational Expertise.* 6.5. May. Pages 275-300. ISSN: 05398–7777

For information on editors (eds.) see page 14

Multiple Authors

Sometimes a host of writers work together on a book. The senior author is still the one the computer will most readily find.

In the text we may put: "Wright et al (1970) give a detailed introduction......" which, in order to get the best results from archive searches, should then be listed in the bibliography in this form:

Wright, D.S. (1970) Taylor, Ann., Davies, D. Roy., Sluckin, W., Lee, S.G.M., and Reason, J.T. *Introducing Psychology. An Experimental Approach.* Harmondsworth: Penguin Books. ISBN: 0 1408 0100 6

The Acid test for all References

The final crunch: Will my reader be able, from what I have given, to find this reference in the library or bookshop.
Of course, there's also the question you do not want to be asking, "Where on earth did I put the details for this reference?"

Editors

There are two types of book editorship you might come across:
- different people write each chapter and the editor brings it all together
- one person has brought together the work of others in a more general way--the names of the individuals don't appear against specific sections of text.

There are also editors of journals—who will be referenced if you quote from their editorial.

In all cases the citing in the text is the same as for all other references:
'In his introduction to mixed ability teaching techniques Wragg (1976) deals with the problem of non-readers."

The listing is:

Editor is shortened to ed. and put in brackets immediately after the editor's name.

Wragg, E.G. (ed.) (1976) *Teaching Mixed Ability Groups.* Newton Abbot: David and Charles Ltd. ISBN: 0 7153 6865 6

Citing someone's chapter in a book edited by someone else.

I recently wrote "If, as Temple (1989) suggests, there is no distinction between specifically open and flexible learning...."

The bibliography listed it this way

*The **book title** is in italic (or underlined)*

Temple, H. (1989) Open learning in a Changing Climate. In Paine, N. (ed.) *Open learning in Transition,* pages 115–25. London: Kogan Page. ISBN: 1 85091 756 6

No date—it's with the cited author

for page numbers some people put pp If you're referring to the whole of the chapter the author wrote you'll put 'Chapter... in....' before the title

When some authors are really stuck for references (the list looks somewhat anaemic) they have been known to cite both the writer of the chapter or pages *and* the editor in the bibliography.

Editions

Popular texts get reprinted and, in some cases, updated. Where the authors rewrite some sections the book is now a *new edition*. (You are reading a third edition, now.) Since each edition has different text it's important to tell your reader to which edition you are referring.

The edition number is inserted in the Bibliography listing after the title of the book. You could have

Bosworth, David P. (2004) *Citing Your References.* (3rd edition). Gilwern: GSSE. ISBN: 0 9527523 4 4

Can be shortened to 3rd ed. Note lower case e

Sometimes the **first named author** changes between editions. In the case of Citing Your References (Bosworth 2004) the author is the same but there's a new publisher. Make sure you've got it all right by copying the information that's on the title page.

Books have an 'information page' that contains all you need for referencing purposes. (For this book it's on the inside front cover.)

Reprints

Where a book is selling well and doesn't need to be up–dated the publishers may simply *reprint* it. This is fine—the bibliographic detail is almost certainly the same as the first printing. *But is it always?* Sometimes the information you quote could be on a different page in the reprint so (while it's not specifically asked for by editors or course tutors) it's as well to give this information—your aim, remember, is to help your readers find a reference you found useful, for themselves.

I suggest

Bland, Michael. (1986) Be *Your Own PR Man* (reprint, first published 1981). London: Kogan Page. ISBN: 0 85038 394 3

Will be on the 'information page'

This avoids any problems a reader might have in finding the exact place you discovered your information.

Cited Works

This is where you are repeating another author's reference to an even earlier piece of work.

For example:
You've read a book and want to include that author's comments about someone else's work in your work. But not in full. Let's say you read this piece:

"... measurement of children's attitudes was carried out by DiVesta(1962) and his co-worker, and by DiVesta (1964,1967) which clearly shows that seven point scales .. ."

You think, 'Right, I can use that information; but I don't want (or need) to go back to the original research. I'll take this writer's word for it.'

Your text will say something like

"In measuring children's attitudes with the semantic differential, Bosworth (1978) shows, using results from Divesta's researches, that seven point scales ..."

The listing is simply for Bosworth (1978) set out in the standard form.

As a general rule
only those works you've actually looked at yourself should be included in the bibliography. Never pretend you've looked back to ancient material — it can be dangerous and is certainly intellectually unsound.

Everyone knows the stories about errors that have been perpetuated because no one bothered to check back to the original data.
Only take the word of someone you can trust.

Reports

Professional, Corporate Bodies

(with no obvious author)

Professional and other corporate bodies produce reports, booklets, pamphlets, even duplicated sheets you may use. There is usually *no obvious author*—the report is by the 'body' itself.

The chairman or secretary of the committee who framed the publication may be mentioned and, in some circumstances, can be listed as the author.

I once referred to a booklet by The Royal Society, with an introduction by 'the secretaries' saying: "The Royal Society (1974) includes all the elements required for an article in their booklet."

In the Bibliography this appeared as

The 'the' is left out of the 'author name'

> Royal Society. (1974) *Notes on the Preparation of Scientific Papers.* London: Royal Society.   *[It doesn't have an ISBN]*

To avoid difficulties in tracing, **The Royal Society** *is filed under* **R** *not* **T.**

Another booklet, which has a foreword and a preface by different, named writers still doesn't have an editor or named author. In the text it has to be referenced as 'The National Extension College (NEC) (1990)' and listed

> National Extension College (NEC). (1990) *Open Learning Moving Into the Mainstream.* Cambridge: NEC. (jointly with CRAC). ISBN: 0 86082 872 7

Note joint publishers—you could decide to list it under **CRAC** *as well*

If in doubt about authorship
  * use the name of the 'body'
  * cross reference   ☞ the NEC booklet above could also be listed as authored by CRAC (the full name is rarely used) if you wanted to be sure your readers would have no difficulty finding it.

Government Documents

If you've ever used government documents for information you'll know they have complicated titles—which have to be given in the bibliography. But they also have names by which they are often known. You will usually have to list them under two or more names.

There are also the code numbers to list — which will be the way experts in government will trace them. Say you want to reference a White Paper on the Future of FE that appeared in 1991 — it's called
> *Education and Training for the 21st Century*

and is coded   *May 1991—Cmnd 1536*

The first part is easy; all government pieces (like white papers) can be listed attributed to *HM Government, making* your listing for this one:

HM Government. (1991) *Education and Training for the 21st Century.* 2 Volumes. CMND. 1536. London: HMSO. ISBN: 0101 153627

If volumes are available separately reference each under its own title

Could be Cmnd.—note the full stop

Government documents are invariably published by the Stationary Office— HMSO is sufficient

ISBN leaves no searcher in doubt

Where documents come from a specific department of government that department can be referred to as the author. Official publications generally have a statement on the title page like:

> "Presented to Parliament by the Secretary of State for Education and Employment and by the Secretary of State for Wales by Command of Her Majesty March 2004".

If such a document existed I would quote it in the text as "in the DfEE (2004) publication we get..." and in the bibliography:

Department for Education and Employment. (1995) *Improving Headteacher Qualifications.* CMND. 954379. London: HMSO. ISBN: 0 101 1536X X

Parliamentary Reports are notorious for the difficulties they cause when referencing and to find from another author's work. They're generally referred to by the name of their Chairman. But, over the years, that person may have chaired a number of committees—and, it's *not the title on the report*. The use of ISBN should make life easier—making tracing the report you're referring to straightforward.

Additions to the UK governmental paper jungle come from

The European Union

When referring to materials from the EU do the same as you would for UK Government materials.

For example, a report produced by the Commission of the European Union (with no obvious author) will be described in the text as 'A report of the Commission of the European Union (1995) describes a number of schemes for small business training' and listed as

Commission of the European Communities. (1995) *Updating for Small and Medium-Sized Enterprises: Experimental Training Schemes.* Sec(88) 2540 final. Brussels: EC.

Their reference (like the UK's Cmnd. number)

European Community Action Programme. (1986) *Teacher Training: Strategies from the Second Transition Programme.* DOC: 35WD86EN. Transition of Young People from Education to Adult land Working Life series. Brussels: IFAPLAN.

This has a different 'author' but can easily be traced by proper use of the EC reference number

All EU documents have a reference number of some sort (not always in the same form if it originates from a different Directorate). Check the information page and, whatever it is, use it!

Also, you may need to specify which *Language* version of an EC document you used. Each one has its own pre- (or suf-)fix to the number: EN in the one above means it's the English language version.

Online Only

Much of your research will revolve around the Internet. You may well find information that is only available online. It may also be possible that what you have discovered is a digital copy of print material. Its referencing leaves you with a number of choices.

Where your findings are digitised traditional essays or books they can be listed in the same way as traditional written materials. However, you may decide to add the online data to your listing.

In citing books or articles found online consider the 'owner' of the Internet site you've accessed to be the publisher. In many cases this will also be the original publisher of material that has been digitised (who will be listed on screen and, of course, you will have printed out);

email can be treated the same as someone sending you a letter—see 'unpublished material' opposite.

Where the material is only available online the URL (universal resource locator) should be given.

A reference where an URL is used could be:

> Library Information Technologies. (1995) *Introductory HTML*. Case: Case Western Reserve University.
> URL: <http://cwru.edu/help/ introhtml/toc.html>

For 'author' I've used the name of the department listed on screen

Try to keep the URL on one line (often impossible for highly embedded articles!)

See the Appendix for additional information about online searches.

> URLs frequently change, go out of business or just disappear. All an author can do is list them and hope!
> NB The < fore and > aft are not strictly necessary but they do show exactly where the URL begins and ends.

Unpublished Material

If you're into the realms of real research you'll be getting a lot of information from duplicated sheets, letters from other researchers, dissertations and theses and so on. There's no problem in mentioning them in the text — it's like all the others, by 'author (writer) and the date' it was written.

{Where letter writers forget to put a date you'll have to list it as 'Smith (undated)'.}

An example of unpublished work:

Bosworth, David P. (1987) Aggression—A Study of Teenagers. Unpublished PhD Thesis. San Rafael: Columbia Pacific University.

This is all you can list.

Perhaps you simply spoke to someone, or a fellow researcher wrote to you with some vital information and you want to acknowledge this. In the text you put 'Name (date)' as usual; in the bibliography it becomes

Bosworth, David P. (1995) Personal Communication.

Maybe you've seen a manuscript on its way to the publisher and you mention something from it. The text won't include a date since the date of publication is still awaited. This is how the text will appear:

"James (in press) has written that ..."
        and the bibliography:

James, John J. (in press) *My Life and All it Holds.*

If you know the publisher who has accepted the script you can add that here — but, **don't guess**

Of course, if it's published before you complete your work you'll have to amend the citation.

Appendix

Researching and Writing

You may photocopy the sample cards (but only the cards) for your own use

Sources

As an author you have goals which include
✔ establishing your credibility in an academic field;
✔ citing all the references you make (plagiarism can be expensive—from non-acceptance of your work, through professional disgrace, to legal action);
✔ readers being able to find books and articles you refer to, or from which you quote;
✔ being accepted as an 'expert'; people seeking out your publications.

As a researcher (before becoming an author) you will want to be sure you have found all the available references relating to the subject on which you are writing.

Tracing the Reference

Your local academic library will give you access to listings of published material (including lists of research programmes) in the form of
books	microfiche
CD-ROM	online bibliographies and listings

Where the author has provided a full citation (as you will) finding a reference is straightforward. The book, journal or article may, then, be
✔ in the library (on the shelf or in the store)
✔ available on inter-library loan
✔ retrievable from an online service.

Searching

It doesn't matter which source you use to trace a reference—the basic rule is the same: *learn how to use the system.*

Every listing has a 'how to use' page; *read this before you start* and work out your search strategy.

When you know the author (or, where there is more than one, the first named) tracing the reference presents few problems. Generally, all the systems also give instructions for carrying out more complex searches.

Which Search Source?

Choosing the best source of listings is part of the research process. Think carefully before you start searching—which source is likely to provide the most useful data for the least time and energy spent searching?

Does the local library have your favourite search tool or easy access to the Internet?
And don't forget half-hidden extras such as *online* surcharges or search fees.

Which Resource?

The 'reference points' in this 'pros' and 'cons' listing should be available in all college/school libraries.

Book

Buy from bookseller; may have updated supplements as part of price.
Does not need ancillary equipment.
Limited to one user at a time; may have to collect, then search, several.
Large, often cumbersome.
Have to copy (or scan in) data found; cut and paste as needed.
Thin pages may give short library life; fiddlesome in use.

Microfiche

Buy from bookseller or specialist suppliers. May be updated with supplements as part of price.
Needs special reader on electricity supply.
Limited to one user per reader.
Fiche easy to store; machines take up desk space.
Have to copy data found and retype for each use.
Easy to damage fiche.

CD-ROM

Buy from bookseller or specialist supplier. May include updates as part of purchase price.
Needs computer with compatible CD-ROM drive and may need additional software.
Any number of computers may be connected to a central server; access depending on the system's capabilities.
CD-ROMs are easy to store.
Data can be copied to own disc and edited or reused directly.
Durable; difficult (but not impossible) to damage; subject to decay.

Online

Buy as you use.

Cost depends on access system and (possibly) time online.

Automatic update.

May include charge for each download or search.

Needs computer, modem, access provider and suitable software (both for access and search).

Any number of access points possible depends on system's capabilities.

On slow access may be cumbersome and expensive.

Data can be downloaded to own disc and edited or reused directly.

Access depends on availability of linkages or system capacity.

Searching correctly

The question you should always ask:- Am I setting about my search In the most efficient way In terms of time, cost and ease of data collection and storage?

Most modern CD-ROMs (and their players) satisfy the international standard ISO 9660, indicating they will work on Mac, Windows and Unix systems.

While most CD-ROMs (and Internet locations) include 'search software' with the data (but it should not be taken for granted). Also they, generally, allow 'interactive searching' allowing you to bring up extra information about items within the text of the initial 'find'.

For all search sources the golden rules are:

Read all the information

Know the search guidelines—download them the first time you log onto the database

Read the instructions in the printed bibliography or on the CD–ROM.

Typesetting Your Publication

The final version of your writing will be composed with a word-processing program giving a wide range of styles and layouts. If you choose your own word-processing package pick the one that covers only what you need. Expensive, sophisticated page lay-out programs are not necessary for most essays, dissertations, journal articles or, even, theses. (And they can add confusing extras you just don't need.)

You will have access to all sorts of type styles (typefaces) and layouts. Don't allow yourself to become hypnotised by them! Keep the style simple with the minimum of typefaces and special effects—just enough to get your message across.

Correcting Manuscripts

Even after using your word-processor's spell and grammar checkers you still need to look carefully at the printout. If you are editing a major piece of work it is as well to use standard proof reader's notation but this will be unnecessary for most class assignments and journal articles. In checking a bibliography you will need to be able to indicate when type should be in
   italic
   bold or
   uppercase (capital letters)
For Example:

THE ORIGINAL	THE FINAL VERSION
This should be in italic	*This should be in italic*
This should appear as bold	**This should appear as bold**
pick out these letters in capitals (Upper case)	Pick out These Letters in CAPITALS (Upper case)
The letters marked should NOT be Uppercase	The letters marked should NOT be uppercase

If something has been printed in italic and it should be 'normal' (the title of an article, for example) mark it like this:

|Computer Supported Co-operative Learning| write |Rom| in the margin

(Rom stands for 'roman' amd means 'use the normal typeface in normal form', in this context.)

Sample Record Card for a Book

Author
Surname,   Forename/Initial.   (Date)   *Title*

_____   _____   _____

_____

Publisher
Place: Name.

_____   _____

ISBN:

_____

Notes

Sample Record Card for a Journal

Author
Surname, _____ Forename/Initial. _____ (Date) _____ Article Title _____

Journal
Title. _____ Volume _____ Number _____ Month _____ Pages _____

ISSN: _____

Notes